faith, hope & love

WHEN THE WORLD IS NOT
AS IT SHOULD BE

CATHERINE DRAEGER-PEDERSON

Faith, Hope & Love
Copyright © 2016 by Catherine Draeger-Pederson

Cover Design by Greg Hahn and Catherine Draeger-Pederson

CreateSpace, Charleston SC

For more information about Catherine Draeger-Pederson visit:
www.LovingVenti.org or www.LinkedIn.com/in/CatherineDraeger

ISBN-10: 0692679030
ISBN-13: 978-0692679036

DEDICATION

Throughout the years of having a broken heart, God was always there. He held me when I had nothing left. He brought restoration and healing to my soul.

To Eric, my husband, who has chosen to enter into life with a once single mom and three children. He shows me every day to live in community with others from various social, economic and racial backgrounds.

To Jonathan, Rebecca and Delila, my three children. May I be an example that even though life may be difficult at times, we serve an amazing God.

CONTENTS

ACKNOWLEDGMENTS

Special thanks to all those who made this Bible study come to life:

… To TJ Lambert and Rebecca Jolin Fredericks for their time and dedication to editing the first draft of this Bible study.

… To Rhonda Miska for her giftedness in putting pen to paper and her time to edit the final draft.

… To Sarah Slagter, Tina Colon-Baldwin, and Kellie Canniff for your attention to details.

… To Greg Hahn for taking my vision for graphics and creating something even better.

… To the women of Oakbrook church (Sussex, WI) who participated the first time I taught this material.

… To my family for letting me curl away on my chair with my laptop to finish.

… To the women of Shielded Hearts who encouraged me along the way. Many of them walked side by side with me on some of the worst days of my life.

… To the Friedens Community Ministries community. For inspiring me to learn about loving those with different family stories.

… To my parents, Greg and Susan Chapman, who were always there to take my kids when I needed a break.

… To God, for giving us the Bible which holds the words to comfort us on our worst days.

introduction

As a little girl, I remember day dreaming about my wedding day. Like many little girls, my dreams were much more like a fairy tale than a realistic event. I dreamed of a day when a man would sweep me off my feet and commit to be mine, from that day forward in sickness and health, for richer or poorer, until death parted us. I would be dressed like Cinderella at the ball and be surrounded by those who loved me dearly.

One thing was non-negotiable: I wanted 1 Corinthians 13 to be read. You know the one. It's typically the exclamation point at weddings, ending with the familiar line, verse 13 'Faith, Hope and Love. But the greatest of these is Love.'

Those three words have been proclaimed as the three pillars of every good Christian marriage. Yet, like many people I know, I would have benefited greatly from a deeper understanding of these words. It would have been helpful to know they were meant for a broader purpose than 'just' weddings; the passage was meant to offer the entire Christian church a way to be different from the world around us. Paul was writing about love in Christian community, not about love between a couple. It teaches us a way to be a community that offers a very real glimpse into the relationship with our Heavenly Father. It is meant to be a breath of fresh air to people desperately longing for more than this world has to offer.

During our struggles we need God's word even more. These are the times that as a Christian community, we need to hold each other up and bear witness to God's great promises.

There are times in our life where Faith, Hope and Love are challenged by looking around and realizing that the world is not as it should be. The words that follow are offered for us to respond whole-heartedly to these times.

ABOUT THIS STUDY

The study that you are about to embark on was birthed out of a time of deep pain. When the life that I knew was turned completely upside down.

It began many years ago as I was writing my master's thesis studying how we are to *Love* our neighbor. I saw so many people wanting to love their neighbors but they did not have the time, energy or understanding of how to fit it into their already busy schedule.

I then dove into what God really says about the promise of *Hope* He gives us when I founded an organization for police families called Shielded Hearts, whose mission is to encourage HOPE in police life. These days *hope* is a buzz word in many organization's mission statements, but I found a hope promised that is so much greater than what the world has to offer.

But *Faith*... that was the hardest, most personal lesson. On March 18th, 2013 my life came crumbling down and I wondered if I had faith enough to get through. That was the day my ex-husband told me he no longer wanted to work on our marriage. My life as I knew it had ended. The chapters that follow grew out of my living and praying through the difficult months after that day.

Join me for six sessions, as we explore together what Faith, Hope and Love look like when the world is not as it should be. As you prepare for each session you'll be asked to read one portion of scripture, investigate the passage, and ponder a few questions.

While this study can be done individually, there is a certain depth of healing that tends to happen in a small group. Each chapter is laid out in two sections. The first section, *Personal Reflection,* is meant to be done before you meet together. The second section, *Small Group,* is designed to walk a group through the passage together. In your small group time, you will further study the passage surrounded by a group of people who can encourage, uplift and pray for each other.

At the end of each section you have space to *Ponder and Pray.* Use this as an opportunity to process any thoughts or emotions that come to mind.

Maybe you are struggling right now. Maybe you haven't completely healed from a pain in your past. Or maybe you are surrounded by others who desperately long to know that there is a God who will not only walk with them, but will in fact carry them when the world is not as it should be.

SMALL GROUP GUIDELINES

To ensure that small group members have the opportunity to engage with each other, your small group should agree upon guidelines. The ones that follow are a recommendation. The role of facilitator is to guide group members back to the scriptures and hold them to the agreed upon guidelines.

Knowing: connecting with each other to create an environment characterized by authenticity and transparency so that group members enter into relationships where we are known, loved, accepted, and challenged.

- ❖ *Attendance & Participation-* Attendance at group functions will be a priority for all group members. We believe that everyone's input to a discussion is valuable. Members are given the right to their own opinions, and all questions are encouraged and respected.
- ❖ *Confidentiality & Trust-* What is spoken in the group stays in the group. We can build trust when this is established.
- ❖ *Openness & Honesty-* Being "real" with God and each other within the group promotes honesty and an ease of sharing feelings, thoughts, struggles, joys, and hurts. This is an imperfect group for imperfect people in an imperfect church.
- ❖ *Acceptance & Unconditional Love-* We will love all members of our group no matter what they have said or done in the past. We understand that every person in this group is at a different point in their walk with the Lord. We will accept you the way you are and at the same time will encourage you to seek Christ's transformation in the future.
- ❖ *Give and Receive Support and Encouragement-* We comfort each other as we are being comforted by God. Supporting others is not giving advice or trying to rescue. It is being willing to listen to a person's story. If we are struggling with a problem, we can usually find at least one other person who has worked through a similar struggle. This person may often be the one best equipped to minister to those striving to overcome similar problems without giving advice.

❖ *Accountability*- In authentic relationships, we voluntarily submit to the accountability of other group member(s) for support, encouragement, and help in a particular area of our lives, giving them some responsibility for assistance in that area.

❖ *Friendship & Fun*- We will strive to build relationships on a personal level with Christ and with each other. We are true friends when we treat others like Jesus would.

Growing: in our knowledge of God and His word, along with connecting in prayer and worship.

❖ *Learning*- Learning about God and about His will for our lives is a key component of group life. We learn about Scripture, one another, and about ourselves.

❖ *Prayer & Worship*- Supporting one another in prayer. We will focus our attention back to the Bible and share personal needs.

❖ *Come Prepared*- For deepening growth please prepare the lesson in advance. This will allow the group to come together with basic knowledge to go further with the study.

Going: each member has something to contribute to those in the group, the community, and the world.

❖ *Open Seat*- We all know people around us who are hurting. This is an appropriate study to encourage them to join you. At any point during the study, new members are encouraged to join and participate. As a group we would make everyone feel welcome and included.

❖ *Contribute*- A small group leader is only one (or two) members of a group. Together we will encourage each other by connecting with other small group members, bringing food, sending notes, praying, and caring for each other.

❖ *Developing our Passions and Purposes*- We will encourage the discovery and application of one's skills and heart's desires so that group members embrace, serve and possibly even bring purpose from parts of their difficult story with people in our small group, local community and the world.

It is difficult to offer such a place [where growth can take place], preciously because we are afraid and find it hard to let the stranger enter our place and reveal to us our own fears. But when we are willing to confess both to ourselves and the other that we too are broken, that we too have a handicap, and that we too need a place to grow, we can build a home together and offer each other an intimate place.

Henri Nouwen

faith

JOINING A LONG LIST

Faith. A word so familiar, yet so often taken for granted. *Faith,* put simply, *is believing in what you do not see.*

For the first 20 years of following the Lord, I never once greatly doubted my faith. But when my marriage was crumbling before me, I questioned if I could hold onto it. I cried out to God, asking why. I struggled with my faith and I wondered if, at the end of this trial, I would still be holding on.

This difficult chapter of my journey of faith began on March 18th, 2013, when my life, as I knew it, ended. I wondered if I had enough faith to press through. It was on that day my ex-husband told me he no longer wanted to work on our marriage. Our marriage, our family, our home, our finances, my career, my ministry, and our public image, had been forever changed in the course of one conversation. Already prone to depression, would I emotionally be able to handle what was inevitably coming for me? I only had one place to turn, God, but… Did I really have faith in God? Did I have faith that God had a plan for me? Did I have faith in what I did not see?

As we open our Bible to the book of Hebrews, we will soon find out that we are not alone. We are joining a long list of individuals whose lives weren't all put together and yet kept their faith. Many of whom never even saw the results of their labor. Many of whom suffered a great deal. Many of whom questioned God. Many of whom are no different than you and me.

Our responsibility is to hold on the best that we know how. Holding on to the promise God has made for us in that He will not leave us. Holding on to the truth that this isn't what God had wanted for His people, but that sin entered the world and tainted His beautiful creation.

Those days and weeks, and even months after my ex-husband told me he was done trying… I lived in a shell of myself. Sometimes I felt like I was holding onto a faith that was as weak as a twig, which could easily break. But I had faith that my marriage would be saved… And yet I am divorced.

However, there was a small voice that wouldn't let me walk away.

HEBREWS 11

¹ Now faith is confidence in what we hope for and assurance about what we do not see. ² This is what the ancients were commended for.

³ By faith we understand that the universe was formed at God's command, so that what is seen was not made out of what was visible.

⁴ By faith Abel brought God a better offering than Cain did. By faith he was commended as righteous, when God spoke well of his offerings. And by faith Abel still speaks, even though he is dead.

⁵ By faith Enoch was taken from this life, so that he did not experience death: "He could not be found, because God had taken him away. "For before he was taken, he was commended as one who pleased God.⁶ And without faith it is impossible to please God, because anyone who comes to him must believe that he exists and that he rewards those who earnestly seek him.

⁷ By faith Noah, when warned about things not yet seen, in holy fear built an ark to save his family. By his faith he condemned the world and became heir of the righteousness that is in keeping with faith.

⁸ By faith Abraham, when called to go to a place he would later receive as his inheritance, obeyed and went, even though he did not know where he was going. ⁹ By faith he made his home in the promised land like a stranger in a

foreign country; he lived in tents, as did Isaac and Jacob, who were heirs with him of the same promise. [10] For he was looking forward to the city with foundations, whose architect and builder is God. [11] And by faith even Sarah, who was past childbearing age, was enabled to bear children because she considered him faithful who had made the promise. [12] And so from this one man, and he as good as dead, came descendants as numerous as the stars in the sky and as countless as the sand on the seashore.

[13] All these people were still living by faith when they died. They did not receive the things promised; they only saw them and welcomed them from a distance, admitting that they were foreigners and strangers on earth. [14] People who say such things show that they are looking for a country of their own. [15] If they had been thinking of the country they had left, they would have had opportunity to return. [16] Instead, they were longing for a better country—a heavenly one. Therefore God is not ashamed to be called their God, for he has prepared a city for them.

INVESTIGATING THE PASSAGE

1. **Underline** each time the word "FAITH" is used in the passage.
2. Double **underline** each time God is mentioned in the passage.
3. **Circle** what each person did because of their faith.
4. **Star** any definitions of faith given in the passage.

Faith, Hope & Love

PERSONAL REFLECTION

DIVING INTO THE PASSAGE

1. In which of life's circumstances did these "ancients" keep their faith?

2. Who else benefited because they kept their faith?

3. Why and how do you think that they continued in their faith when they didn't see immediate results?

> The apostles said to the Lord, "Increase our faith!" He replied, "If you have faith as small as a mustard seed, you can say to this mulberry tree, 'Be uprooted and planted in the sea,' and it will obey you. In the hard times do you truly have faith that God is with you? Luke 17:5-6

4. Write your definition of faith based on the above passage.

5. For more stories of faith keep reading…
   Hebrews 11:17-40

DIVING INTO YOUR LIFE

7. What moments in your life have you lived by faith? What is one "leap of faith" you have taken?

2. What did you hope would happen or think you would see during those times?

3. How have you known/felt/seen God intertwined in your faith story? How has God been faithful to you?

4. Fill in the following…

By Faith _____ (your

name) _____ (action word:

believed, called, understood, taken, built, obeyed, trusted,

etc…),   even   while   going   through

_____ (painful/difficult time). With

God,   there   was   still   hope   and   assurance   of

_____(promise).

*Write this on a notecard and post it somewhere that you
will see it regularly and be reminded of God's goodness.*

SMALL GROUP

INTRODUCTIONS

Pretend you are being interviewed for a 30 second commercial. Share your name, details of family and work, and a fun fact. Try to 'leave us hanging,' and wanting to know more. Give us something we can ask you about later.

RE-READ SCRIPTURE OUTLOUD (Hebrews 11)

ANOTHER LOOK AT THE PASSAGE

1. As a group, share the background (from the Old Testament) of some of those mentioned in this passage.

Resource: a few examples are listed in the leader's notes at the end of this book. Also refer to your Bible's footnotes or consult a commentary.

2. What might have happened if they chose not to live by faith?

3. Does it seem unfair that they never were able to see all the results of their faith? Why?

4. How are faith and hope tied together in this passage?

5. Share your definition of faith with the group.

CONNECTING

Each of us has a story of faith. We've all had difficult times of struggle in our lives. In those times, we all chose to do or believe something, though we didn't know the end result. In your group, please share one of your faith stories. Other members should listen without intersecting, interrupting, or offering advice.

PRAYING FOR EACH OTHER

Lord, thank you for not leaving us alone in our struggles. While we go through some very difficult times, You show us through Your Word, through the ancients, that You were there with them... and You are, and will be there for us. On our worst days, You have a plan and a promise for us that we have yet to see. We wait on You for a better place, and a heavenly peace.

PONDER AND PRAY

_____

_____

_____

_____

_____

_____

_____

_____

_____

_____

_____

_____

These were all commended for
their faith, yet none of them
received what had been
promised, since God had planned
something better for us so that only
together with us would they be
made perfect. Hebrews 11:39-40

Now faith is confidence in what we
hope for and assurance about what
we do not see. Hebrews 11:1

_____

_____

_____

_____

_____

_____

_____

_____

_____

_____

_____

_____

_____

_____

_____

_____

_____

_____

_____

_____

_____

_____

Why did Christ pray specifically for Simon Peter's faith not to fail? Peter's future was not dependent upon a perfect track record. It was dependent upon his faith. Peter would desperately need the courage to believe he was still who Christ said he was even after such failure.

Beth Moore

faith

HOLDING ON AT A CROSSROAD

It is so easy to doubt that God really wants the best for you when you see a mountain in front of you. This mountain could be a seemingly unconquerable rock of pain, disappointment, fear, sickness, financial ruin, death, and/or loneliness. A mountain can seem so large that it feels we could never climb the elevation to get over the peak. Yet these are the very times that God asks us to have faith in Him. Trust Him. He can and does do so much more than we imagine. That mountain in front of us is nothing compared to the absolute power He holds in His hands. While the mountain seems large now, in one moment, He could slide it into the sea.

Do you believe this could happen? In the midst of my deepest, darkest pain, I struggled. While I knew in my *head* that God wanted me to have faith, my *heart* only saw the steep pitch in front of me. It was hard to FEEL the faith.

Divorce is expensive in many ways: physically, emotionally, financially and spiritually. Most mountains in life deplete one, if not all our resources. It's a cycle that seems like a downward spiral. One area of expense, such as financial, leads to emotional fatigue, so on and so forth.

While I was still emotionally, spiritually and physically exhausted, I knew if I wanted to keep a roof over my kids' heads I was going to need a job. For the seven and a half years prior, I had poured my heart into Shielded Hearts, an organization that I founded, but also an all-volunteer movement. However, I needed a JOB.

I was so tired, I didn't know how I would gather enough energy to keep going. Self-doubt plagued me. Could I get a job based on skills I knew I had, but had never been paid to use? In May, as I was looking over my finances, I knew I could handle things until July 1st, but then I'd need help to pay my bills. After applying for over 90 jobs, June 1st came and went with no prospects. In three months of job searching, I only had two phone interviews.

This mountain before me looked like it would crush me. But my faith had a contingency plan. I knew I would have the ability to waitress, babysit and do a thousand side jobs to keep my kids fed. I've heard it said that one should 'work as if everything depends on you, pray as if everything depends on God.' But, in this case, I had a weak faith that I'd have a job July 1st. Yet that is exactly what happened. Through God's providence and my perseverance, I was employed using the very skills I had built while volunteering all those years.

In less than a month's time I applied, interviewed and was offered a job that joined my passions and skills. When offered the job, they said, "we know it seems CRAZY, but if possible we'd really like you to start in less than a week. We would really like you to start July 1st." God is faithful!

MARK 11

²² "Have faith in God," Jesus answered. ²³ "Truly I tell you, if anyone says to this mountain, 'Go, throw yourself into the sea,' and does not doubt in their heart but believes that what they say will happen, it will be done for them. ²⁴ Therefore I tell you, whatever you ask for in prayer, believe that you have received it, and it will be yours. ²⁵ And when you stand praying, if you hold anything against anyone, forgive them, so that your Father in heaven may forgive you your sins."

INVESTIGATING THE PASSAGE

1. **Underline** each time "faith" and "believe" are used in the passage.

2. **Circle** each time the passage refers to prayer.

3. Put a **Star** in the passage next to that which you think would be the most difficult to have faith (in times of doubt, belief, prayer, forgiveness, etc...)

PERSONAL REFLECTION

DIVING INTO THE PASSAGE

1. How are faith and belief connected?

2. How are faith and prayer connected?

> Faith is the only thing that will ever close the
> gap between our theology and our reality.
> ~Beth Moore

3. How difficult is it to throw a mountain into the sea? How is this related to doubt?

4. Can you think of other examples in scripture when people had extraordinary faith and God moved their mountain or He rewarded them for it?

DIVING INTO YOUR LIFE

1. Do your prayers ever seem too big, too unbelievable, too unrealistic to be answered?

2. What hinders your faith?

3. Why is it so hard for us as humans to believe?

4. Do you remember a time in your life that someone promised something and didn't follow through? Is there ever a time you made a promise and didn't follow through? Describe.

5. How did it make you feel?

6. How do you think this affects your relationship with God?

SMALL GROUP

INTRODUCTIONS

What is the most amazing sight you have ever physically seen (moment in time, a part of God's creation, or a man-made wonder)?

RE-READ SCRIPTURE OUTLOUD (Mark 11:25-28)

ANOTHER LOOK AT THE PASSAGE

7. What had happened right before this passage that led to Jesus responding to the disciples with a passage about faith? (Matt 11:1-21)

2. In your group, share other examples in scripture when people had faith, and how God answered them.

CONNECTING

1. Why is it so difficult to have faith to move a mountain or even a mole hill?

2. Why does forgiving others help YOU have faith?

3. What secondary emotions or feelings do you experience when you sustain your unforgiveness?

4. Think back to the story of faith that you shared in lesson one. Is there a mountain in the middle of your past or current faith story which you would love to see moved?

PRAYING FOR EACH OTHER

Lord, this mountain before me seems unmovable and insurmountable... but to You, it is something that you could easily throw into the sea, if it is Your will. Please help me out from under my disbelief, help me trust the plan You have for my life, and remind me daily that I can really come to You in full faith and without any doubt. If I am holding onto unforgiveness or bitterness that won't allow me to see You clearly, please help me forgive as You forgave. Allow me to see You at work in my life when mountains are before me. Help me to look above the mountain to You, who can see the other side.

PONDER AND PRAY

Therefore, since we are surrounded by such a great cloud of witnesses, let us throw off everything that hinders and the sin that so easily entangles. And let us run with perseverance the race marked out for us, fixing our eyes on Jesus, the pioneer and perfecter of faith. For the joy set before him he endured the cross, scorning its shame, and sat down at the right hand of the throne of God. Consider him who endured such opposition from sinners, so that you will not grow weary and lose heart. Hebrews 12: 1-3

Truly my soul finds rest in God;
my salvation comes from him.
Truly he is my rock and my salvation;
he is my fortress, I will never be shaken.
How long will you assault me?
Would all of you throw me down—
this leaning wall, this tottering fence?
Surely they intend to topple me
from my lofty place;
they take delight in lies.
With their mouths they bless,
but in their hearts they curse.
Yes, my soul, find rest in God;
my hope comes from him.
Truly he is my rock and my salvation;
he is my fortress, I will not be shaken.

Psalm 62:1-6

hope

WHAT GOOD IS SUFFERING?

We are surrounded by people desperately looking for a glimmer of hope. We say to our friends and family that we *hope* to see them soon. Our churches paint the word *hope* on their walls. Our stores sell decorations with the word *hope* to hang throughout our homes. Our nonprofits use it as part of their mission statements. Even those in marketing try to convince us that their product will give us hope for a better tomorrow.

Yet all these messages fall short. They may give temporary relief. They are a small glimmer of light beyond our current circumstance. At the end of the day, they leave us longing for more. They leave us wondering if there IS more. Are you curious if God's Word leaves us with an answer?

I wrote the letter below to the 275 members of Shielded Hearts the week after my ex-husband had told me he was divorcing me. It broke my heart to step down as the Executive Director of a ministry that I had founded. And honestly, it was pretty humiliating to do so. I felt that I had failed myself, my family, the police wives of Shielded Hearts and the mission that was before us to Encourage Hope in Police Life.

Dear Shielded Hearts Members,

When you hear that there is a 75% divorce rate in police marriages, you always hope and plan to be one of the 25% of couples that beats the odds. You still feel the stress of the job. You still have your ups and downs. But no one is totally unaffected. Yet some stay together against all odds.

Unfortunately, my husband and I have been going through years of struggles. Our struggles are one of the reasons I poured so much of my life into finding hope in police life. I knew that law enforcement relationships were tough. I wanted to do everything I could and find every possible resource out there; books, speakers, friends who have been there before, praying often to God for guidance and strength, etc... I knew I longed for a better marriage. And just as I was desperate to have God and fellow police wives bring hope to my life, I wanted to do the same for others.

Yet right now it looks like we will not be defeating the odds. We both understood that there were problems in our marriage, yet I still had hope one day things would be better. One doesn't really plan for the day where one realizes that it's done. No one really thinks it's going to happen to them.

. . .

It amazes me that Shielded Hearts started with a cup of coffee just over six years ago. The journey has not always been easy and there have been times when we wanted to give up. Yet it is because of ALL of you that we have really become a community of women encouraging hope in police life!! And we HAVE made a difference!! As I step down I intimately know the importance of our vision of encouraging hope in police life. There are too many hurting individuals, couples and families out there who need your help in stepping beside them wherever they are on this journey.

. . .

As you can imagine I'm not doing well emotionally, physically and spiritually. It has been an incredibly difficult week. I don't have any clue where I will be working, living or really how this whole process works.

I do ask that you please respect both my husband and I in this process. He is amazing at what he does at work. He is a really good police officer. He is an amazing dad. We just had our problems communicating and showing love in a way that the other understood.

Please pray for me as I step out on my own. I ask you to pray for our children, the ones who will suffer the most. I am trusting that it is my God who will sustain me. It is He who will dry my tears. It is He who will guide and direct my paths. At this time of unrest I have been meditating on the verse: 'Trust in the Lord with all of your heart, lean not on your own understanding. In all of your ways acknowledge Him and He will make your paths straight.' I cannot see the straight path right now but my God has been faithful in the past and I know He will again.

Encouraging Hope in Police Life,
Catherine Draeger

As I re-read the letter that I wrote, I am amazed that from the beginning I had a glimmer of hope even in the darkest days of my life. But my journey of hope didn't start that day… it was already woven in my spiritual DNA. My exploration of what hope meant came when I was founding Shielded Hearts and as we were praying about the organization's vision. At the end of the day, what we wanted more than anything else: we wanted to be able to Encourage Hope in Police Life. But what is hope? I desperately wanted more than what the world had to offer. Everything those around me promised seemed to fall short. So I dove into what God's word said. In EVERY case the Bible says that hope is in GOD… or in the LORD. Every time!

ROMANS 5

[1] Therefore, since we have been justified through faith, we have peace with God through our Lord Jesus Christ, [2] through whom we have gained access by faith into this grace in which we now stand. And we boast in the hope of the glory of God. [3] Not only so, but we also glory in our sufferings, because we know that suffering produces perseverance; [4] perseverance, character; and character, hope. [5] And hope does not put us to shame, because God's love has been poured out into our hearts through the Holy Spirit, who has been given to us.

INVESTIGATING THE PASSAGE

1. **Circle** those words in the passage which, to you, mean hope.

2. **Underline** those words in the passage which, to you, mean pain.

3. **Star** each mention of God, Jesus Christ or the Holy Spirit.

PERSONAL REFLECTION

DIVING INTO THE PASSAGE

1. What is the one thing in which we can boast?

2. In what ways does this passage mention hope?

3. When going through a time of suffering, why does hope not let us be put to shame?

4. Write your own definition of hope.

DIVING INTO YOUR LIFE

Time after time, we may read this passage without realizing how real this example is in our lives. Please contemplate some specific examples in your life.

1. Suffering produced Perseverance…

2. Perseverance produced Character…

3. Character produced Hope…

4. What does hope produce in your life?

5. How has God poured His love into your heart?

SMALL GROUP

INTRODUCTIONS

As a child, I'm sure we all looked forward to Christmas morning when our living rooms were filled with festive decorations and presents piled under the tree. Share one gift that you remember hoping you'd get. Why was it so special?

RE-READ SCRIPTURE OUTLOUD (Romans 5:1-5)

ANOTHER LOOK AT THE PASSAGE

Think about places in scripture where we have examples of people who experienced the following:

1. Suffering producing Perseverance…

2. Perseverance producing Character...

3. Character producing Hope...

4. Products of hope?

5. Share your definition of hope with the group.

6. Who should have been filled with shame but instead God poured His love out to him? How has God poured His love into your heart?

7. Read Romans 4:18-25 which leads into this passage. How do the sins that one commits fit into the message of hope?

8. How does one's faith intersect with the message of hope?

9. Why would shame be a normal response to our sin?

Shame: isn't it that when we are suffering we think that we are in a shameful situation? I'm sure Abraham may have felt some shame that he did not have a son to carry on the family name. Often suffering is surrounded by shame.

10. When shame is a normal response, why would God pour out His love for us?

CONNECTING

1. Think about the messages of hope marketed to us. What slogans, mission statements or signs have you seen around you with HOPE as their objective? Share some of them that come to mind.

2. Was there a time in your life when all seemed hopeless? Please share.

3. Can you share a time in your life when you saw the process go from suffering to perseverance to character to hope to a concrete experience of God's love poured into your heart?

PRAYING FOR EACH OTHER

Lord, You are the One in whom we can place our hope. You are not like the shifting sand that changes with every tide. But You are a stable rock that we can trust for our firm foundation. When we are going through times of suffering, it is sometimes difficult to imagine that we will get through the day, much less have something good come from it. Yet we come to You longing for more. Sometimes we come to You with all that we have, we come to You with just a small seed of faith, with a small bit of hope. Draw us to You, even when it seems difficult to see beyond that which is in front of us. Help us to be willing to go through a time of perseverance in order to let You build our character. Let us fully experience the hope You offer, and Your love poured into our hearts.

PONDER AND PRAY

You see, at just the right
time, when we were still
powerless, Christ died for the
ungodly. Very rarely will
anyone die for a righteous
person, though for a good
person someone might
possibly dare to die. But God
demonstrates his own love for
us in this: While we were still
sinners, Christ died for us.
Romans 5:6-8

Faith, Hope & Love

_____

_____

_____

_____

_____

_____

_____

_____

_____

_____

_____

_____

_____

_____

_____

_____

_____

_____

_____

_____

_____

_____

_____

_____

_____

God says there is no hope for the world aside from the cross. We look to the leadership of men, the progress of scientific discovery, or the spread of knowledge and think human beings can find solutions to our problems. But our hope rests not in a system, or a government, or a philosophy, but in the cross of Christ.

Billy Graham

For I know the plans I have for you, declares the Lord, plans to prosper you and not to harm you, plans to give you hope and a future.

Jeremiah 29:11

hope

OVERFLOW

I tumbled to the ground, sobbing. Such a rush of emotions overcame me. I'm honestly not sure which left me a puddle on the floor: the news that my husband was leaving me or the unknown of how I could possibly move on. Days turned into weeks, and I still felt like a walking zombie. I know that it was only because of God's grace, and friends and family surrounding me that my kids were fed each day and that my house kept some sort of order. Left on my own, I would have been so inoperative that I wouldn't have had the wherewithal to even realize that I felt so hopeless.

I don't think joy or peace were in my emotional vocabulary during those first couple of months. Getting out of bed was often a lofty goal. But, little by little, through pain and tears and sounds which came out as prayers, a small flame of trust was flickering. I began to trust that God knew more than me.

He, who had been there for me before, was STILL there. It took many months before a spontaneous smile would spread across my face. It was an even longer wait for a sense of inner peace. It seemed like an eternity to experience true hope. God didn't leave me to sob on my kitchen floor. He had much more in store for me.

How many of you have ever felt hopeless? The hopelessness that seems so overwhelming that there just seems no possible way out. The hopelessness that doesn't seem to ever go away.

Maybe it feels like you are in a tunnel and no matter what direction you look, you see nothing but darkness. You sometimes try to lift your heavy legs to move, because anywhere seems better than where you are at. Sometimes you just curl in a warm, dark corner to retreat from life.

But there was hope, even when I couldn't get off the couch for days. For my God of Hope, by the power of the Holy Spirit, was my hope when I had none of my own. I trusted Him at that time, trusting that while each day was hard, something good would come of it.

And we know that in all
things God works for the
good of those who love him,
who have been called
according to his purpose.
Romans 8:28

ROMANS 15

[13] May the God of hope fill you with all joy and peace as you trust in him, so that you may overflow with hope by the power of the Holy Spirit.

INVESTIGATING THE PASSAGE

This week I'm asking you to do something different. Please try to memorize Romans 15:13. If memorizing things are difficult for you, write it out on several index cards and place it in your bathroom, your car dashboard and your purse.

PERSONAL REFLECTION

DIVING INTO THE PASSAGE

What other verses in scripture mention the word Hope? Feel free to look it up in the foot notes of your bible, the leader's notes at the end of this study, quote verses you have from memory, or even search online for it.

DIVING INTO YOUR LIFE

1. Envision moving through your day with a life filled with "joy and peace." What is it like to get out of bed, go through your routine, interact with family, friends, and colleagues?

2. Why do you think that God asks us to trust Him?

3. Does God ask us to just get by, or does He want to fill us to the point of overflowing? Does this seem an attainable goal in your life? Or are you wanting to believe it, but struggling to get through the day? Explain.

4. Which verse about hope is your favorite? Why do you connect with it?

SMALL GROUP

INTRODUCTIONS

Have you seen someone go through something terrible with a confident attitude? Maybe you've watched a grandmotherly figure bravely battle an illness, or a mother who handled the death of a child with supernatural grace, or a friend who responded with peaceful confidence to a job loss. Please share your experience, and what you've learned from these examples.

RE-READ SCRIPTURE OUTLOUD (Romans 15:13)

ANOTHER LOOK AT THE PASSAGE

Some of us are better than others at finding scripture passages on specific themes. Please spend some time together, looking up and reading the passages that others in your group have found. Talk about how our lives would look if we took to heart and believed every message of hope found in our Bibles. Write down a few passages that you want to return to ponder later.

CONNECTING

1. Honestly, how do you really feel when you watch someone else's happiness, while your life seems to be falling apart?

2. What are there tangible things in life that give you joy and peace?

3. Please be an inspiration to others in the group and share about a time in your life when you knew God was giving you an abundance of hope.

4. Was there a time that your overflow of hope allowed you to care for someone going through a similar struggle?

PRAYING FOR EACH OTHER

Lord, You promise to fill us to the point of overflowing, with the hope that can only come from the Holy Spirit. Some days, joy and peace are two of the furthest thoughts from our minds. On those days, Lord, honor our baby steps. We long to let You fill us with Your hope and Your love. Give us the strength to trust You when we can barely figure out what we should be doing in five minutes. While we may not see it today, help us trust that one day we will not just read about You filling us with joy and peace, but that we truly experience it!

PONDER AND PRAY

_____

_____

_____

_____

_____

_____

_____

_____

_____

_____

_____

I consider that our present sufferings
are not worth comparing with the
glory that will be revealed in us. For
the creation waits in eager
expectation for the children of
God to be revealed....

For in this hope we were saved. But
hope that is seen is no hope at
all. Who hopes for what they already
have? But if we hope for what we do
not yet have, we wait for it patiently.

Romans 8: 18-19, 24-25

LOVE DEEPLY: Do not hesitate to love and to love deeply. You might be afraid of the pain that deep love can cause. When those you love deeply reject you, leave you, or die, your heart will be broken. But that should not hold you back from loving deeply. The pain that comes from deep love makes your love ever more fruitful. It is like a plow that breaks the ground to allow the seed to take root and grow into a strong plant. Every time you experience the pain of rejection, absence, or death, you are faced with a choice. You can become bitter and decide not to love again, or you can stand straight in your pain and let the soil on which you stand become richer and more able to give life to new seeds. The more you have loved and have allowed yourself to suffer because of your love, the more you will be able to let your heart grow wider and deeper. When your love is truly giving and receiving, those whom you love will not leave your heart even when they depart from you. They will become part of yourself and thus gradually build a community within you. Those you have deeply loved become part of you. The longer you live; there will always be more people to be loved by you and to become part of your inner community. The wider your inner community becomes, the more easily you will recognize your own brothers and sisters in the strangers around you. Those who are alive within you will recognize those who are alive around you. The wider the community of your heart, the wider the community around you. Thus the pain of rejection, absence, and death can become fruitful. Yes, as you love deeply the group of your heart will be broken more and more, but you will rejoice in the abundance of the fruit it will bear.

The Inner Voice of Love ~ Henri Nouwen

love

LOVING OTHERS IN PAIN

As the pit of depression weighed on my heart, the last thing on my mind was the pain of those around me. My pain kept blinders on my eyes so I could not see the pain of others.

The more I focused on me, the more I went into the depths of despair. After a while this place became comfortable. It was easy to get wrapped up in my own pain thinking it was the only thing that mattered. I tried to convince myself that I was wronged and deserved to wallow in it. But at the same time I wanted out. I wanted freedom. I wanted my life back.

For myself, I found that the more I narrowed the focus to my pain, the more it consumed me. However, on those rare occurrences when I was graced with the ability to walk with another in pain, I myself also found healing and comfort.

We are often so busy, self-absorbed, or just haven't realized that our greatest mission field is the one between our own two feet.

Jesus said the second greatest commandment is to, "Love your neighbor as yourself" (Matt 22:39). At first glance, we might think this is an easy commandment to follow. We would all like to 'be nice to each other,' and it's the culturally correct thing to do. As my grandmother would say, "We don't want to ruffle any feathers."

But is "being nice" all there is to loving our neighbor? Did Jesus make a point to make sure we love the Lord our God with all our heart, soul, and mind... and then, 'by the way, in your free time,' love your neighbor, too? No, he instructs those who call themselves Christians to love God, their neighbors, and themselves. It begs the question: why are there so many of us in the world who are lonely, hurt, struggling, hiding from the world and crying ourselves to sleep?

If we, as Christians, truly loved our neighbors, what would it look like? I'm not talking about new initiatives or government programs. I'm thinking about what we can do now to live out this commandment and make a difference to those already in our lives. We have no control over what others do, but if we could make a difference in just one neighbor's life, how powerful could that be?

You see, *faith* and *hope* are primarily about our personal relationship with Christ. Our faith and hope is our lifeline to the Creator. Faith is our foundation. Hope is distinctive of the Christian life. But *love*... love is first about our relationship with God, AND then our relationship with people around us. It is a visual, tangible way to show others what God has poured into us. People are hurting around us every day. What can "WE" possibly do? How can "WE" possibly love others in pain?

LUKE 10

25 On one occasion an expert in the law stood up to test Jesus. "Teacher," he asked, "what must I do to inherit eternal life?"

26 "What is written in the Law?" he replied. "How do you read it?"

27 He answered, "'Love the Lord your God with all your heart and with all your soul and with all your strength and with all your mind'; and, 'Love your neighbor as yourself.'"

28 "You have answered correctly," Jesus replied. "Do this and you will live."

29 But he wanted to justify himself, so he asked Jesus, "And who is my neighbor?"

30 In reply Jesus said: "A man was going down from Jerusalem to Jericho, when he was attacked by robbers. They stripped him of his clothes, beat him and went away, leaving him half dead. **31** A priest happened to be going down the same road, and when he saw the man, he passed by on the other side. **32** So too, a Levite, when he came to the place and saw him, passed by on the other side. **33** But a Samaritan, as he traveled, came where the man was; and when he saw him, he took pity on him. **34** He went to him and bandaged his wounds, pouring on oil and wine. Then he put the man on his own donkey, brought him to an inn and took care of him. [35] The next day he took out two denarii[c] and gave them to the innkeeper. 'Look after him,' he said, 'and when I return, I will reimburse you for any extra expense you may have.'

[36] "Which of these three do you think was a neighbor to the man who fell into the hands of robbers?"

[37] The expert in the law replied, "The one who had mercy on him."

Jesus told him, "Go and do likewise."

INVESTIGATING THE PASSAGE

1. **Circle** each of the people mentioned in this passage.
2. **Underline** each of the ways the man on the side of the road was helped.
3. **Star** anything that stood out to you (an amazing, surprising, odd, or a-ha moment).

PERSONAL REFLECTION

DIVING INTO THE PASSAGE

1. What is the most important question asked in this passage?

2. Describe the Teacher of the Law.

> The Theological Dictionary of the New
> Testament defines a neighbor as the one
> "who is closest to the one in need of help."

3. Describe the Man left on the side of the road.

4. Describe the Priest and Levite.

5. Describe the Samaritan.

No one has ever seen God; but if we
love one another, God lives un us and
his love is made complete in us.
1 John 4:12

DIVING INTO YOUR LIFE

1. Identify those people you come in contact with on a regular basis, such as your physical neighbors, close friends, fellow health club members, work associates, parents or teachers at school, etc.

2. What modern day circumstances or life problems may our neighbors be going through that could be equivalent to this man being left for dead on the side of the road?

3. Why is it difficult to approach such a person?

4. What can we say to someone when they are so hurt, when they feel "half naked?"

5. What does it feel like to be that person left alone on the side of the road?

6. How do you react when you see others in pain?

Let's be honest, we have all crossed to walk on the other side of the road: we've ignored a text, let a call go to voicemail, and half-listened to a person in need of a sympathetic ear. We've even typed a quick, "praying for you," with no real intention of follow-through. We've judged too quickly or we've pitied others. We've assumed that we have no tangible way to help, so we do nothing.

7. Does the image of your neighbor change if you remember that he/she is also created in God's image? Read Psalm 139:13-18

If we think of our neighbors, those around us, as a beautiful mosaic of what God looks like, our impression of others change.

SMALL GROUP

INTRODUCTIONS

Share with those around you what you would do if you had a day to yourself, assuming you had everything on your To-Do list already done!

RE-READ SCRIPTURE OUTLOUD (Luke 10)

Spend some time going over the questions in Diving into your Life, especially questions 2 and 3.

DIVING IN TOGETHER

/. In what ways did the Samaritan show mercy and help the man found on the side of the road?

2. How can we have mercy on our "neighbor"?

> When God asks us to give him something, he asks us to give him only what we already have. It might take a little work to identify what that is, but we already have what we need to help move others closer to him. The problem is we don't think that what we have is enough.
> ~Jim Henderson

> Whatever you did for one of the least of these brothers of mine, you did for me. Matt 25:40

3. Is there something practical you can ask someone to help you with in the coming week?

4. What would happen if someone took a few moments out of his/her busy schedule to show you mercy?

5. On a grand scale, what could happen if we lived out this commandment and made a difference in the lives of those with whom we come in contact, despite our own busy schedules?

6. Before you leave, write down how you can help one specific 'neighbor' this week.

PRAYING FOR EACH OTHER

Lord, when we are so busy and focused on ourselves, it's difficult to see the pain of others. When we do see it, we sometimes wonder if or how we can help. Some problems seem so large that we don't want to get involved. Others seem insignificant compared to our own. And other people seem to have it all together, so we wonder if we are even needed. But Lord, You ask us to love our neighbors as ourselves. So open our eyes this week and show us how we can, with our time and resources, help others. Father, forgive us for the times we have just walked by. Give us the vulnerability to show others how they can love us, before we are left on the side of the road. Help us accept help from others, as we are letting them obey Your commandment when we do. Thank you Lord, for caring for us through the hands and feet of the neighbors around us.

PONDER AND PRAY

_____

_____

_____

_____

_____

_____

_____

_____

_____

_____

_____

_____

_____

_____

_____

And let us consider
how we may spur one
another on toward
love and good deeds.
Hebrew 10:24

_____

_____

_____

_____

This is how we know what love is: Jesus Christ laid down his life for us. And we ought to lay down our lives for our brothers and sisters.
1 John 3:16

Praise be to the God and Father of our Lord Jesus Christ, the Father of compassion and the God of all comfort, who comforts us in all our troubles, so that we can comfort those in any trouble with the comfort we ourselves receive from God. For just as we share abundantly in the sufferings of Christ, so also our comfort abounds through Christ. If we are distressed, it is for your comfort and salvation; if we are comforted, it is for your comfort, which produces in you patient endurance of the same sufferings we suffer. And our hope for you is firm, because we know that just as you share in our sufferings, so also you share in our comfort.

2 Corinthians 1: 3-7

love

LOVE IN A BROKEN WORLD

How often have you heard 1 Corinthians 13 read at a wedding ceremony? It's a great passage that can inspire a great marriage. But the truth is, this passage wasn't meant to limit itself to that relationship alone. Paul is actually writing this entire letter to the church in Corinth. In this section, he was asking the church to love each other better. Why? Because it's a testimony to the world of the love that God has shown them. Jesus was the ultimate example of love: dying on the cross. The church was to love when they were hurting. They were to love the unlovable. They were to love in a way contrary to what was happening around them.

Has your marriage dissolved like mine? Have you found yourself bankrupt? Are you sitting day and night in a hospital room with a loved one? Have you lost a child?

I have chosen to love again after such great loss. I have allowed myself to open my heart to the most vulnerable places again. I have taken a risk, knowing that I may open myself up to more pain in saying that the "greatest of these is love"… once again. Even in the midst of a broken world. Why? Because I see that's what God modeled for us.

When Paul writes that we are to live with, 'faith, hope and love, but the greatest of these is love,' it's not that it's the greatest in our relationship with God. Faith in God is obviously very important, hope is life-changing, but our love for others is what sets us apart from everyone else.

As we go through the passage, we find that too often we fall short of Paul's teaching. The side effect of falling short is that we end up hurting the broken. We minimize others' pain. We highlight one sin over another. We judge. We boast. We lose our patience. Instead, we need to love as He loved.

I was so scared to walk into church Sunday after Sunday when my ex-husband left me. I was humiliated, yes, but I was so scared of being judged. I feared that my walk with The Lord would be questioned. That my friends would turn a cold shoulder to me. That I wouldn't be given the opportunities to serve Him. In worship. In leading a nonprofit or ministry. Or even here writing this now.

And what about when I started dating again? Would I be judged that it was too soon? Would I have evil eyes on me for not waiting for my ex-husband to change his ways and return?

We live in a culture that teaches us to sugarcoat our own pain and yet put a spotlight on others. Although my pain was very public, in many cases other's pain is much more hidden.

1 CORINTHIANS 13

[1] If I speak in the tongues of men or of angels, but do not have love, I am only a resounding gong or a clanging cymbal. [2] If I have the gift of prophecy and can fathom all mysteries and all knowledge, and if I have a faith that can move mountains, but do not have love, I am nothing. [3] If I give all I possess to the poor and give over my body to hardship that I may boast, but do not have love, I gain nothing.

[4] Love is patient, love is kind. It does not envy, it does not boast, it is not proud. [5] It does not dishonor others, it is not self-seeking, it is not easily angered, it keeps no record of wrongs. [6] Love does not delight in evil but rejoices with the truth. [7] It always protects, always trusts, always hopes, always perseveres.

[8] Love never fails. But where there are prophecies, they will cease; where there are tongues, they will be stilled; where there is knowledge, it will pass away. [9] For we know in part and we prophesy in part, [10] but when completeness comes, what is in part disappears. [11] When I was a child, I talked like a child, I thought like a child, I reasoned like a child. When I became a man, I put the ways of childhood behind me. [12] For now we see only a reflection as

in a mirror; then we shall see face to face. Now I know in part; then I shall know fully, even as I am fully known.

[13] And now these three remain: faith, hope and love. But the greatest of these is love.

INVESTIGATING THE PASSAGE

1. **Circle** all the examples of love, both positive and negative.

2. **Underline** each time you find the words: tongues, prophecy, faith, give and knowledge.

3. **Star** any particular items in which you've been hurt.

PERSONAL REFLECTION

DIVING INTO THE PASSAGE

1. How does this passage compare prophesies, tongues, knowledge, etc. to love?

2. What does this passage say will happen in verse 8:

Love:

Prophecies:

Tongues:

Knowledge:

3. List all the characteristics of love.

DIVING INTO YOUR LIFE

1. What is so attractive about a group of people that shows this type of love to one another? When have you experienced this? When have you shown this kind of love?

2. How can withholding love from one another bring division into a group of people? When have you experienced this?

3. Why do you think that love is being singled out as being greater than faith, hope, tongues, prophecies, knowledge, giving, etc...?

4. Which of the characteristics of love in this passage is hardest for YOU to live out? Why?

SMALL GROUP

INTRODUCTIONS

Tell a story about when you felt most loved. It could be from your childhood or adult life.

RE-READ SCRIPTURE OUTLOUD (1 Corinthians 13)

CONNECTING

7. Your church may or may not practice tongues and prophecies on a regular basis. What are some things you do that look strange to people unfamiliar with your church service?

2. We can easily share stories about other people who have not loved others well and who are not great examples of how we are to love one another, but this would only lead to dishonoring those individuals and keeping records of wrong. Yet we are responsible for ourselves. Are you willing to share a personal example of how you have hurt others because of how you withheld love from them?

Our church is supposed to be a safe place for those who have been struck by the world when it's not as it's supposed to be... and yet often the church kicks their wounded. Often we do it with good intentions, because we want to make sure people know that we are holy and don't tolerate sin... that while my sin stinks, it doesn't stink as bad as yours.

Paul is telling us that love is what lives on... love is what the outsiders can see... love is what makes a body of believers attractive... Loving others is a tangible way showing the love that was first shown to us. Love is not for those who want to act like children, but those who have grown up. Love allows us to be fully known.

3. Share a positive ripple effect in your life when someone showed you love?

4. What would the church be like if it practiced each of these love characteristics among its' members?

5. Would you want to attend such a church? Why?

6. Reflect together about how faith, hope and love can still exist when the world is not as it should be.

PRAYING FOR EACH OTHER

Lord, we have come together week after week to see how faith, hope and love can be lived out when the world is not as it should be. We have seen from Your Word that You are with us during our greatest struggles. You comfort those who do not see the results of their faithfulness. You long to fill us with the hope that comes through the love. You pour out into our lives. You want us to experience love through those around us. We know this isn't a journey that a magic pill can heal. Rather, it is a journey that may take days, months or years. But You ask us to trust in You. You ask us to put our faith, hope and love into You, who can carry us through every bad day, and whose presence can overflow to those around us.

PONDER AND PRAY

_____

_____

_____

_____

_____

_____

_____

_____

_____

_____

_____

_____

_____

_____

No one has ever seen
God; but if we love
one another, God
lives in us and his
love is made
complete in us.
1 John 4:12

conclusion

For I know the plans I have for you, declares the Lord,
plans to prosper you and not to harm you, plans to give
you hope and a future.
Jeremiah 29:11

Ultimately, the world is not as it should be. We live in a broken world where people have chosen their own wisdom over the wisdom God offers us. The wisdom of the world often leads to sin and pain. The wisdom of God leads to life everlasting.

I have come a long way from the eight year old girl dreaming of a fairy tale wedding, being whisked away by my prince, but I have come to the other side of finding something much richer, much deeper.

We choose faith, hope and love so that the world has an opportunity to see Jesus through us. This is what separates Christians from non-Christians. What kind of testimony are you giving others by living your life, even when you go through difficult times? Let us live our lives knowing that we will encounter pain, but won't lose *faith*; lives that may not know what tomorrow brings, but won't lose *hope*; lives that could hold a grudge, but instead choose *love*. Amen!

As we go from here, let us look to the One who promises that His message of Faith, Hope and Love is not just to be read on our wedding day but lived every day, especially when the world is just not as it should be...

Taste and see

Taste and see that the LORD is good;
blessed is the one who takes refuge in him.
Psalm 34:8

I imagine that there are a few people who have gone through this study and are still not sure about what it means to be a Christian. Looking for faith, hope and love is a longing in the hearts of both non-Christians and Christians. I would encourage anyone who is not sure of their next steps to "taste and see that the Lord is good" (Psalm 34:8.) God has so many more ways to comfort us than can possibly be shared in one Bible study. Keep going. Pick up another book. Read the book of John in the New Testament. Talk to a Christian friend. Ask God for faith in what you do not see.

*Jesus said that he came "that they may have life,
and have it to the full"
John 10:10*

PONDER AND PRAY

_____

_____

_____

_____

_____

_____

_____

_____

_____

_____

_____

_____

_____

_____

_____

_____

_____

_____

_____

_____

_____

_____

Faith, Hope & Love

PONDER AND PRAY

PONDER AND PRAY

PONDER AND PRAY

_____
_____
_____
_____
_____
_____
_____
_____
_____
_____
_____
_____
_____
_____
_____
_____
_____
_____
_____
_____
_____
_____
_____

LEADER'S NOTES

INTRODUCTION

As you begin together, you will be stepping into a new community of people who are coming together, perhaps for the first time. As the leader, you are privileged to facilitate a group of people who long to be in God's word and supported by Christian communities. There may be some in your small group who are nervous and scared about diving deep with others on such painful topics. Yet as the leader, your job is to create a safe environment where people are able to share. As the leader, you should model vulnerability and share from your own painful experiences. This is not to boast in your pain, but to set an example to others. This study has been designed to slowly ease people into this process of opening themselves to the group. Follow the guide to lead you deeper into God's word and community with each other.

During your first time together review the Small Group Guidelines on page 13.

While you are preparing for each gathering together, remember to pray for those who will attend. Bringing up pain stirs up emotions that we often ignore. Our tendency is to cover up pain and suffering and come to church with a smile pasted across our face. This group is intended to be a bridge to those two worlds. No one person can do this life alone, we need God to be at work and comfort those whom He has entrusted into our care.

FAITH: JOINING A LONG LIST

Scripture Background: Hebrews 11:1-16

Hebrews 11 continually looks back to stories of Genesis.

Vs. 3 Creation of the World: We're not exactly sure of all the specifics of creation, but somehow God created everything from what was not visible – All of creation benefited – Genesis 1

Vs. 4 Abel: Brought a better offering to God than brother Cain – Yet Cain killed Abel and went on to get married and have children – Genesis 4

Vs. 5 Enoch: Pleased God so he didn't experience death – We know little about Enoch, except that he was in the lineage of Adam and one day was no more. – Genesis 5:18-24

Vs. 7 Noah: Built an Ark – He looked like a fool when building an Ark with no rain in sight – Genesis 6:9 – 9:17

Vs. 8 Abraham: Promised Land - Followed God without knowing the plan, often times his story involves things that don't seem like he believed God had a plan – Genesis 12-25

Vs. 11 Sarah: Abraham and Sarah were told that their descendants would become a great nation, yet she was old and still childless – Woman of faith, yet she laughed at God – Genesis 15 (Promise), Genesis 17:15-22 (Abram laughs), Genesis 18:10-15 (Sarah laughs), and Genesis 21 (Birth of child)

Vs. 13 Insight into those who are called "faithful." Yet upon further study you will see that each person was longing for a better tomorrow.

Hebrews keeps going… Sharing stories about Abraham, Isaac, Jacob and Esau, Joseph, Moses' parents, Moses, people passed through the Red Sea as on dry land, walls of Jericho which fell, Rahab the prostitute, David and Samuel, etc… Yet the common theme is that they all had faith even though they didn't see what was promised to them.

Group Background

We are to live by faith... financially, emotionally, physically, spiritually, in our relationships and in life itself. During your first session together explore the differences between your expectations that come to mind when you think of the word faith and what you read in scripture. After spending time in God's word, share how your expectations connect with your experiences in your everyday life.

Review Introduction and Small Group Guidelines.

FAITH: HOLDING ON AT A CROSSROAD

Scripture Background: Mark 11:22-25

As Jesus was in Jerusalem, the chief priests and teachers of the law were looking to kill him. At the same time, Jesus was disappointed because the temple courts had become a den of robbers. In the middle of all of this a fig tree that Jesus and his disciples passed had no fruit, so he cursed it. When they passed it the next day Peter exclaimed "Rabbi, look! The fig tree you cursed has withered! (Mark 11:21)

Our scripture today is Jesus' response.

Group Background

Explore how our relationships with other people affect our thoughts about faith. Pay special attention today that the group doesn't turn into a complaining session. People will always fail us: that's why we need to turn to God. If possible, focus on those times that God did answer.

HOPE: WHAT GOOD IS SUFFERING

Scripture Background: Romans 5:1-5

The passage leading up to today's text refers back to Abraham's faith in God, fulfilling His promise of Sarah becoming pregnant while she was old. The cycle found in Romans 5:1-5 starts and ends with God. In the middle you find pain and peace, suffering and joy. Which is all wrapped around a message about how God has poured his heart out for those that love Him.

Group Background

By now, members of your small group will have begun to share their personal stories. What a great honor it is to walk with someone in their pain; as you look at the effects of suffering this week people may focus on shame rather than hope. There is a time and place for both, but as a leader, please gently guide them to the hope that the passage offers.

HOPE: OVERFLOW

Scripture Background: Romans 15:13

Ultimately, God's plan is to reconcile us with Him and each other. The more that we focus on Christ, the easier it is to accept one another.

A sample of other passages on hope:

Jeremiah 29:11 "'For I know the plans I have for you,' declares the LORD, 'plans to prosper you and not to harm you, plans to give you hope and a future.'"

Psalm 39:7 "But now, Lord, what do I look for? My hope is in you."

Hebrews 11:1 "Now faith is confidence in what we hope for and assurance about what we do not see."

Romans 12:12 "Be joyful in hope, patient in affliction, faithful in prayer."

Hebrews 6:19 "We have this hope as an anchor for the soul, firm and secure."

Matthew 12:21 "In his name the nations will put their hope."

Group Background

There are times that we look around us and everyone looks happy, we are than led to think we are the only one with problems and this brings us great pain. We can allow this shame to cover our emotions and not allow them to be released. It is highly likely that this is the first time for someone in your group to feel comfortable sharing a deep pain. Listen to their story. Be careful about judging them or giving them advice. Instead, memorizing scripture allows us to meditate on something positive over and over even if at that moment we don't feel it. At some point it will fill us with hope, which leads to joy and peace even on our worst days.

LOVE: LOVING OTHERS IN PAIN

Scripture Background: Luke 10:25-37

Teacher of the Law: Knowing the rules doesn't always lead to good actions. As the teachers of the law they knew what they needed to do, but also how to get out of jobs that they would rather avoid.

Priest and Levite: These guys normally get a bad rap in this story. Truth is that they may partially deserve it. But if I'm honest, I may be in their shoes more than I'd like to admit. They are Godly men who know if they get close to the half dead men then they will not be able to do their job and lead others in worshipping God. They would need to be separated from the community for a time of cleansing.

Samaritan: A people group who would have been despised by the Jews.

Inn Keeper: Often forgotten. The Samaritan was not to be left alone to take care of the half dead man. Whether he needed to work, take care of his family, or had other life situations to attend to, he pulled in a care team.

Half Dead Man: He lost all physical positions, his health and his dignity. He was alone. He could not have saved himself. He was dependent on others.

Group Background

After four sessions of focusing on our own pain, we shift our focus to the pain of others. We learn that in this world we all have something to offer and we all have something to receive. This isn't meant to guilt us into serving others, but to open our eyes that it doesn't need to be that overwhelming to make a difference. While loving people is difficult, it is also beautiful. People will hurt you. They want you to accept them. They want you to be real. To offer hope in the daily minutes of life.

Before you leave, encourage each person to think of one thing that they can do this week to love someone else. Next week, ask them about it!

(For more information on ways to love the people in your life visit: www.LovingVenti.org)

LOVE: LOVE IN A BROKEN WORLD

Scripture Background: 1 Corinthians 13:1-13

Our passage this week is sandwiched in 1 Corinthians as Paul is teaching on the church. He pauses to help remind these church planters to not forget the purpose. Tongues, prophecy, knowledge, and proper church etiquette are important to church life but *love* is the tangible sign of God's presence to those outside the church.

Group Background

This is the last session of the Bible study. By now, we hope that everyone in your group has shared part of their story. Perhaps some have even expressed that they have never experienced a Bible study where they felt so open to share. But we are not done. This last chapter ties everything together. We are looking at a familiar passage in a new way. You will look at the "love is" passages in context of the church body. There is a lot that could sting. Even preparing this study I felt the stings of pain that I've experienced being in the church. The church is a place that we expect to be free from hurt. It is to be more loving. And yet at times, those outside of the church sometimes love people better than we do. Don't focus your time on "fixing" the church, it does no good to criticize others. My prayer is that your group has grown together and visibly been the examples of the "love is" expressed in this chapter to one another. Help your group today continue to think about what our world would look like if the church showed this type of love to one another.

Finish with the 'conclusion' and 'taste and see'... They are a great way to wrap up the study. Encourage your group members to take the next step in their faith journey: whether pursuing further healing; joining another bible study; or continuing to meet together.

NOTES

Henri Nouwen, *Lifesigns* (Garden City, New York.: Doubleday, 1986), 34. (p. 7)

Beth Moore, *Believing God* (Nashville, Tennessee.: B&H Publishing Group, 2004), 77. (p. 25)

Beth Moore, *Believing God* (Nashville, Tennessee.: B&H Publishing Group, 2004), 21. (p. 30)

www.ShieldedHearts.org (p. 44-45)

Billy Graham, *Hope For The Troubled Heart* (New York, New York: Bantam Books, 1993), 64. (p. 61)

Henri J. M. Nouwen, *The Inner Voice of Love* (New York, New York: Doubleday, 1996), 59-60. (p. 77)

To become a part of a community intentionally empowering people to love people visit: www.LovingVenti.org (p. 80)

Gerhard Kittel and Gerhard Friedrich, *Theological Dictionary of the New Testament Vol. VI,* (Stuttgart, Germany.: Wm. B. Eerdmans Publishing Co.; 10th edition, 1984), 72. (p. 83)

Jim Henderson, *Evangelism Without Additive.* (Colorado Springs: WaterBrook Press, 2007), 75. (p. 90)

ABOUT THE AUTHOR

Catherine Draeger-Pederson has been an Executive Director and Nonprofit Entrepreneur for over 10 years. She has empowered movements of people to love the 'neighbors' all around them. Yet it was Catherine's most difficult times both professionally and personally that fueled her desire to write and speak from an open heart.

Catherine has received numerous awards including the *Ten Outstanding Young America's* (TOYA) award in 2015 from the United States Junior Chamber (Jaycees). She earned her Master's Degree in Christian Studies from Trinity International University. Her article *Between My Feet* was published in *Just Between Us* magazine.

Catherine enjoys reading a good book, listening to Christian singer songwriters, traveling, becoming a slow and steady long distance runner, serving those around her and visiting local coffee shops with friends. She lives in Milwaukee, WI with her husband, Eric Pederson, and three children.

www.LinkedIn.com/in/CatherineDraeger

LOVING VENTI

Empowering people to love people
& bring purpose from our broken cups

Catherine has combined her passions of leading nonprofits, sharing her brokenness and watching others share the hope found in Jesus into the organization Loving Venti.

www.LovingVenti.org

www.ingramcontent.com/pod-product-compliance
Lightning Source LLC
Chambersburg PA
CBHW060937040426
42445CB00011B/905